Tying
Bugs and Flies
for Bass

Other books by A. D. Livingston

The Sky's the Limit
Poker Strategy and Winning Play
Dealing with Cheats
Fishing for Bass
Advanced Bass Tackle and Boats
Fly-rodding for Bass

Tying
Bugs and Flies
for Bass

by A. D. Livingston

J. B. LIPPINCOTT COMPANY
Philadelphia and New York

U.S. Library of Congress Cataloging in Publication Data

Livingston, A D birth date
Tying bugs and flies for bass.

1. Fly tying. 2. Black bass fishing. I. Title.
SH451.L58   688.7'9   77-23196
ISBN 0-397-01187-3

**For
Frankie**

Contents

Illustrations

Numbers are page numbers.

Preface

It's more fun to fool a fish with an artificial lure than to catch one on natural bait, and it's even more fun if the lure was made by the angler's own hand.

There is also the matter of quality. With a little practice and some patience, you'll be able to make better bass flies and bugs than you can purchase at the usual bass tackle outlets. Fishing with a well-made lure is of itself a source of pleasure.

Further, the bass angler who creates his own flies and bugs instead of using off-the-shelf lures or copying another man's design will know that he is fishing with a lure that is like no other. I might add that the black bass is a versatile feeder and is, it seems, often looking for something new.

In any case, fly-tying is a highly satisfying hobby in its own right, and beginners would do well to start with bass flies and bugs, or perhaps saltwater flies, simply because they are large and easy to handle as compared to many of the tiny trout flies.

Good luck. And good fishing.

PART ONE

Cork, Balsa, and Plastic Bugs

1

Easy Bugs

SOME OF MY FAVORITE BASS BUGS are dressed with neither hair nor feathers, and they require no tying whatsoever. I'm talking about bugs fitted with either rubber or vinyl skirts. Such skirts are available in tackle shops or can be ordered from some of the mail-order houses listed in the appendix of this book. Although it is sometimes difficult to locate skirts in the smaller sizes, it is usually permissible to cut long skirts off. As a rule, the skirt should be about 1½ times the length of the bug's body—but I frequently use skirts of longer proportion.

The body of the bug can be made from cork or balsa, or even from such materials as Styrofoam. (Body design and construction will be discussed more fully in the next chapter.) The easiest and quickest way for the beginner to proceed,, however, is to buy some preslotted cork bodies from the supply houses. These are available in a variety of sizes and shapes. Be sure to order long, hump-shanked hooks in sizes specified for the cork bodies. The humped shank helps prevent the hook from turning in the slot. Of course, heavy cement or glue is also required. I prefer epoxy mixtures, but ordinary glue squeezed from a single tube is more convenient. Plastic wood, liquid "steel," and other such compounds can be used more or less successfully.

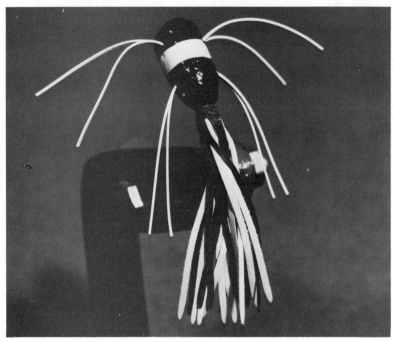

Great bass catchers like this can be made without feathers, hair, or even thread.

The basic procedure for making easy bugs is illustrated in the photographs. Note here that the skirt attachment will slide down onto the hook's bend if it isn't secured. The skirt can be snugged up to the bug's body and wedged against the hook's shank with trimmed toothpicks, matchsticks, and so on. Alternate methods include carving or otherwise shaping a hump in the rear of the bug's body, or inserting a round-headed pin into the rear of the bug immediately atop the hook's shank. You can even pinch a split-shot sinker onto the hook's shank, but the shot tends to work loose if you change skirts a few times or fish the bug pretty hard. The best bet is to form a permanent bead or hump from epoxy putty.

You can also build up a hump with fishing line, tying thread, or small lead wire. The lead works nicely if you want the tail of the bug to sit low, giving the bug a different (and sometimes effective) action. If you use any sort of wrap-on hump, be sure to saturate the windings with glue so that the hump won't unravel.

In short, a skirt can be more or less secured to the hook's shank by a number of methods, but I recommend using epoxy putty as illustrated in the photographs.

I prefer rubber skirts instead of vinyl, especially if I am going to fish the bug very slowly with gentle twitches and long pauses. A rubber skirt has a subtle, enticing action even when the bug's body is sitting dead in the water. The strands of rubber straighten out when the bug is twitched, then curl up slowly when the bug is at rest. If a bass is a little leery of your offering and lays off to watch the bug instead of striking, this leg action might do the trick. Drop a new rubber skirt into a glass of water and watch it do its thing. But rubber skirts must be of top quality and should be kept in good condition; heat and improper storage will kill a skirt's action and may even melt the strands into a most wretched mess.

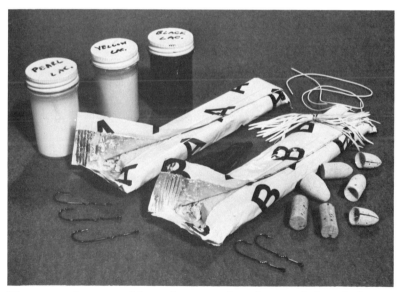

The materials required for making easy bass bugs include only hump-shanked hooks, corks, rubber hackle, skirts, and paint.

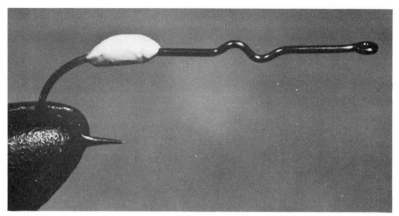

Begin by forming an epoxy putty head on the hook's shank. The epoxy should, of course, be mixed according to the manufacturer's instructions. Moistening your fingertips slightly will usually help in forming the bead. After the epoxy sets thoroughly, it can (if desirable) be sanded down or otherwise shaped with sandpaper or cutting tools.

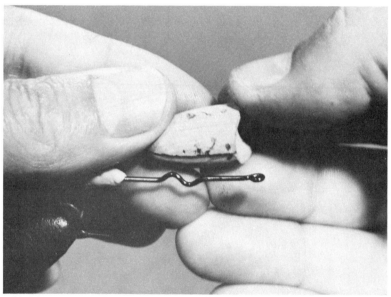

Then glue a slotted cork body onto the hook. The slot should be completely filled with a good glue, and, of course, the hook and the cork body should be pretty well matched to each other.

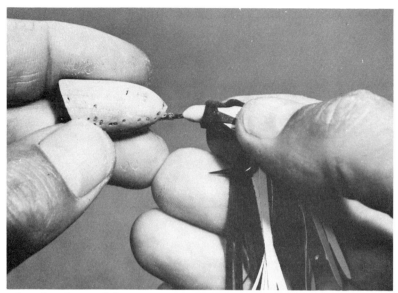

After the glue and the epoxy putty have dried and set, attach a rubber or plastic skirt over the bead. If the skirt won't go on fairly easily, sand the epoxy bead down a bit. After the skirt has been attached, the bug can be fished as is, but almost all anglers will want some paint on the cork body, and many will want to add some rubber legs.

I know some anglers who simply will not use a bug unless it has rubber legs sticking out on either side of its body. I've even heard one bassman say that it doesn't matter what kind, color, or shape of bug you use, as long as it has legs on it. I wouldn't go that far, but I too am fond of legs.

Rubber hackle, as it is called, isn't normally available in tackle shops, but it can be ordered from most of the supply houses. I prefer rubber hackle in small diameter because it is more supple. I'm thinking not only of leg action in the water but also of the finished bug's castability. Thin rubber legs fold back on the cast, thereby holding air resistance to a minimum.

Special needles with hook eyelets are available for use with rubber hackle. The idea, of course, is to thread the hackle into one side of the bug's body and out the other. Although many

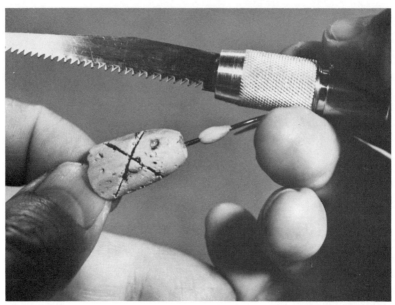

There are several ways to apply rubber legs to bass bugs, but my favorite method is to saw crisscross slots in the cork body, as shown above. Then rubber hackle is glued into the slots, as shown below. The legs will stay in place better if you knot the hackle before inserting it into the slots.

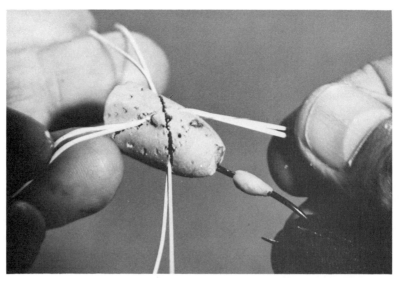

commercial bugs have legs attached in this manner, I don't recommend the method. Too often legs will pull out, or you may end up with a leg longer on one side than on the other. Also, it is difficult to get needles in and out of the bug's body symmetrically, and errors can cause the bug to tilt in the water.

The better way, in my opinion, is to saw slots into the bug's body and then glue the legs in place. Slits can be made with razor blades or sharp knives, but it is difficult to get glue into such a slit. I prefer to use a saw with fine teeth to make the slot.

I normally go in from the top and cut down to about midway of the bug's body. It is also all right to make the cuts from the underside of the bug's body, and I use this method from time to time.

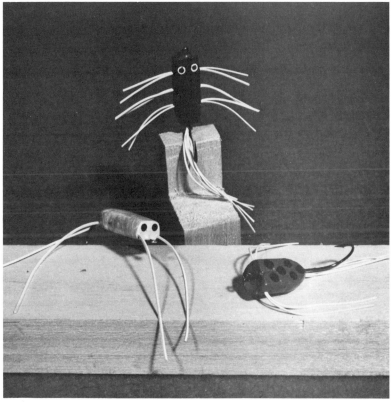

Bass bugs dressed only with rubber hackle.

The big problem with rubber legs is that the diameter of the hackle becomes smaller when the legs are stretched from either side. Even if you glue the legs into slots, the contraction causes the hackles to slip. I've tried rubber cement, Goodyear's Pliobond, and other types of glue without much success. The best bet, in my experience, is to tie overhand knots in the strands before gluing them in. Then use epoxy. One problem with gluing in legs (and hooks, too) is that the bug's body may soak up the glue. This is especially true with bodies made of balsa. It will help if you apply a coat of good sealant and let it dry thoroughly before gluing in the hackle. The sealant can be applied with a small brush, but be sure you don't clog up the slot. The best bet is to saturate a strand of heavy yarn with sealant, insert it into the slot, and remove it after a couple of minutes.

As shown in the accompanying line drawings, there are several patterns for rubber legs. (Note also that rubber hackle can be used for a bug's tail.) I prefer to use a crisscross pattern because it makes the legs more spiderlike instead of merely sticking straight out.

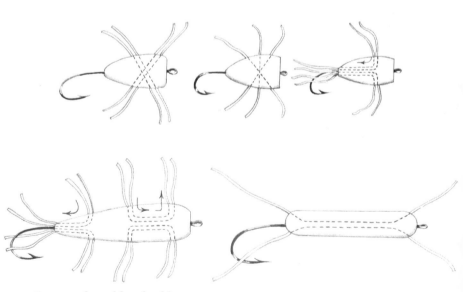

Patterns for rubber hackle.

2

Designing and Making Bug Bodies

A FUNDAMENTAL REQUIREMENT for a good bug is that the body and hook be right for each other. A bug must have bite. If the hook is too short for the body, or if its gap isn't wide enough, a good many strikes will be missed. The general rule (as shown in the accompanying diagram) is that the hook's point

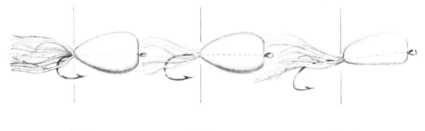

Bad   Better   Best

Matching body and hook.

should never be forward of the rear of the bug's body. This rule should always be followed, but other factors bear on the matter.

A bug's hooking ability also depends on how fat the body is, as well as on the length of the hook in relation to the length of the body. Usually, a flat-bottomed bug with the hook positioned low will be more efficient than a fat bug with the hook running through the center of the body.

Most of the mail-order catalogs recommend hook sizes for the various cork bodies listed. These recommendations are generally about right, but beginners can go astray. Most such recommendations are based on a double-humped, long-shank (3X) hook. Specifically, it's the Mustad 33903. Other hooks may not be as long, and therefore will not work effectively.

McNally Green Frog, made by Jim Poulos. This is a bug with bite! It was designed almost thirty years ago by Tom McNally, who said, "Incidentally, I'm the one who originated the idea of extra-long, 3X hook shanks in popping bugs, and mounted at a *near-40-degree angle downwards* so that fewer strikes are missed."

Eagle Claw's Keel hooks can be used to make durable bugs, but I've never puzzled out a way to make these so that the hook's point rides up. Hence, the Keel bugs I've made were not weedless (except for hair bugs). But I'm sure there is room for experimentation in this area. If you want to try your luck with Keel hooks, I suggest the No. 2 streamer hook; the saltwater Keel hooks are too heavy-duty, and you'll have trouble sticking them into a bass.

Here's a bug tied on a bent-shank Keel hook from the Keel Fly Company. It is weighted a bit so that it sits almost vertically in the water.

Some of the other bent-shanked hooks may also have potential. In fact, a fellow named Bill Hutchison makes his excellent Pad Popper bug on the Mustad 3777 central-draught hook. The Pad Popper is weedless and is therefore covered in chapter 4, page 58.

As I have said, bodies for bass bugs can be made from cork, balsa, and other materials. Cork is no doubt the most common body material, and it does have several advantages. It is light. It is tough and resilient, so that hooks won't rip out too easily. It is impervious to water. And it is readily available. Reed's and some of the other supply houses market preshaped slotted bodies, as well as tapered and cylindrical corks. Also, corks of various sizes and shapes can be purchased from tackle shops and hardware stores. And don't overlook the use of cigar-shaped cork floats.

Cork-bodied popper by E. H. Peckinpaugh Company, whose founder, Ernest H. Peckinpaugh, made the first cork-bodied bugs in the early 1900s.

Ka-Boom-Boom Popper tied by the author. Created by Elwood "Cap" Colvin, this bug is made by cutting a cigar-shaped fishing float in half, at a 45-degree angle. Try it.

Commercial bass bugs are usually made from cork, but a few craftsmen do work with balsa, a material that has advantages and disadvantages. It is very light, and bugs made from it have a certain bouncy buoyancy. Balsa isn't pitted like cork is, and it can be shaped into sleek bug bodies. Preshaped balsa bodies are not available, but the material is easily worked with hobby saws, knives, and sandpaper. Balsa blocks and strips in various lengths and sizes can be purchased at most hobbby shops.

The problem with balsa is that it isn't as tough as cork. Unless the finish is very hard and tough, a fish can bite into a balsa bug, and it is not easy to bond a balsa body to a hook satisfactorily. Merely gluing a humped-shank hook into a piece of balsa won't work too well. The body will turn on the hook's shank under pressure. The glue may hold, but the balsa itself breaks loose inside the slot.

Another method is to make a hole through the balsa body instead of sawing a slit. (Such a hole can be made with a drill bit

Balsa bug by Poul Jorgensen. The hook is mounted in a hole running through the body.

or with a small rat-tail file.) Then wrap a suitable hook with chenille. (The chenille should be wrapped tightly and should cover
a portion of the hook's shank as long as the bug's body.) Saturate
the chenille with a good glue, insert the hook into the hole, and
then let the assembly dry thoroughly. This method seems to
work better than gluing a bare hook into a slot, simply because
the chenille increases the surface area of the balsa involved in
the stress areas, thus distributing the load more evenly, and
over a larger area of balsa.

Personally, however, I have trouble drilling a hole straight
through the balsa body. For this reason, I usually make my own
balsa bugs by gluing humped-shanked hooks into slotted bodies.
Bugs made in this manner last well enough if you're careful
when unhooking your bass.

Balsa is easily worked with knife, saw, or abrasive aids such
as sandpaper. Cork is a tad more difficult to work, and for this
reason it is best to purchase bodies that are more or less preshaped. Cork cylinders can be tapered pretty easily with

Balsa is easily shaped with small hobby saws and sandpaper.

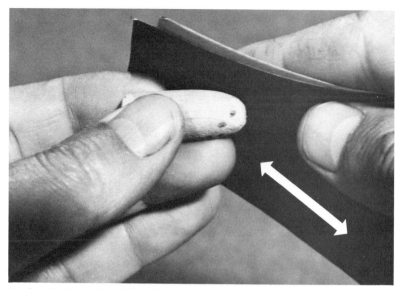

Cork cylinders should be shaped with sandpaper or emery cloth.

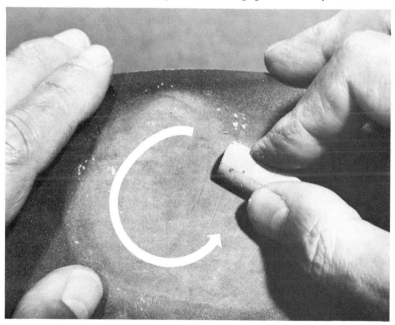

Flat-bottomed bugs can be made by grinding cork cylinders down on sandpaper or emery cloth.

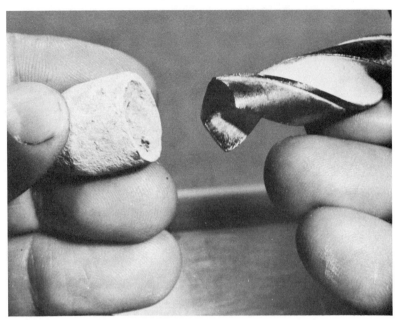

Dished-out bug faces can be shaped with rotary cutting tools. The author often uses an ordinary drill bit, hand held.

sandpaper or emery cloth. To make flat-bottomed bugs, place a sheet of sandpaper or emery cloth on a smooth surface and work the bug's body in a circular motion while applying a slight downward pressure. Bug faces can be slanted by the same method.

A good, fine-toothed saw be used to rough out flat-bottomed bodies or slanted faces, but the cuts should then be smoothed down with sandpaper.

Popper faces can be dished out with various rotary bits made for electric drills. These can be either abrasive bits or bits with a steel cutting edge. I often use ordinary drill bits of ⅜- or ½-inch diameter. You can, of course, use the bits in an electric drill, but sharp bits will cut nicely enough when used by hand—which is much safer.

Cedar and other woods can be used for making bug bodies, too; in fact, some of the better saltwater bugs are made from

Saltwater skipping bug tied by Bill Gallasch. These are sometimes made from cedar.

cedar. Such woods are heavier than balsa and cork, and aren't as easy to work—but they do make a stronger bug.

Hard plastics are sometimes used for commercial bass bugs, but these are made by a molding process that just isn't practical for do-it-yourselfers. One possibility is to buy hard plastic bodies affixed to hooks and tie on your own dressing.

It is possible to make bug bodies from Styrofoam and similar material, which can be obtained from the packing used to ship TV sets, radios, and most small electrical appliances. This stuff can be cut roughly with knives, saws, or even scissors, then finished with sandpaper. Many of the better glues, however, will melt Styrofoam, so do a little experimenting. I use epoxy putty. Whatever glue you use, a body made from foamy materials won't last long. But they are easy to make, they are very light, and they cast nicely. And they'll catch fish.

33 / *Designing and Making Bug Bodies*

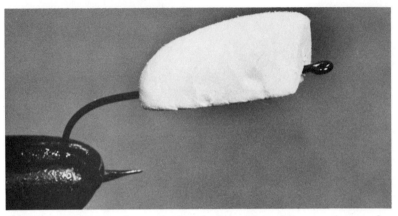

Styrofoam can be used to make bug bodies. These bugs aren't very durable, but they are light and easy to cast and have more bounce even than balsa.

Foam-rubber bug bodies, available in either floating or sinking models, are widely available from the supply houses. These are usually dressed only with rubber hackle, spiderlike. Various sizes are available, but most of them are a little too small to suit me. They *will* catch bass, though—if you can keep the bluegills off them. (Try a fast retrieve.) The hook can be threaded through the foam-rubber body, but this is rather difficult, at least for me. I usually slit the body from the underside and insert a hump-shanked hook. Then I glue the slit shut after the rubber legs have been wrapped on.

Some bugs pop and burble in the water on the retrieve, some slide along, and some fall between these two extremes. Some bugs tend to dive on the pickup, and others lift off. Which design is best should depend on the fishing conditions. If I were fishing murky water, I would probably choose a popper; if I were fishing clear, shallow water, I would probably choose a slant-faced, flat-bottomed bug that could be picked up and presented gently. In the first case, the idea is to get a bug that will attract bass; in the second, to get a bug that won't frighten or spook the bass.

Cork, Balsa, and Plastic Bugs / 34

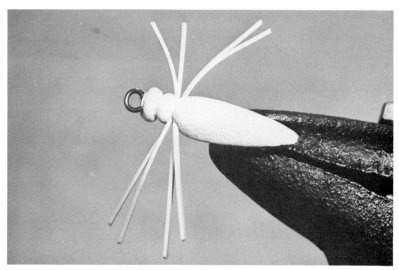

On rubber spiders, the legs are tied in from either side. The thread used to bind the rubber hackle also helps bind the bug's body to the hook. Additional windings at the head and between the head and the legs give a "thorax" appearance to the spider and also add strength.

Diving Demon by Gaines. This design will catch lots of bass, but it is difficult to get out of the water on the pickup.

The following notes are keyed to the diagram illustrating some of the bass bug body designs:

1. Poppers have a dished-out face and make an acoustical blast when they are jerked or sharply twitched in the water.

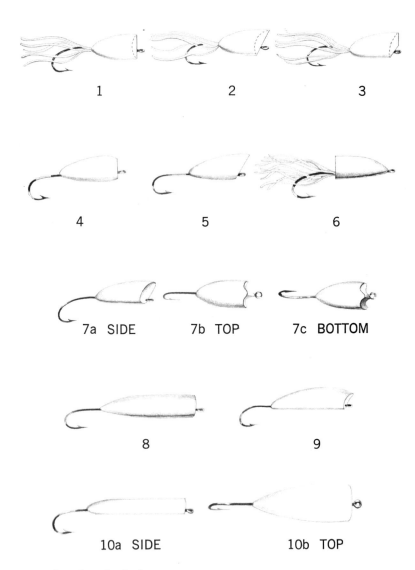

Some bass bug body designs.

This design is quite popular and has taken many a bass. But bugs made by this design tend to dive on the pickup and therefore aren't ideal from a casting standpoint.

2. This popper has a slanted concave face. It doesn't tend to dive as strongly as design 1, and it can be picked up a little easier.

Popper by Boone Bait Company. An excellent design.

3. This design is a compromise between 1 and 2. I like it.

4. Flat-nosed bugs will plunk and burble on the surface, but they don't pop quite like poppers. I call these "pushers" because they tend to push water ahead instead of producing a downward acoustical blast.

5. This design is more of a plunker than 4. When fished fast, however, it can be made to skip along the surface effectively, and it is sometimes called a skipping bug.

37 / Designing and Making Bug Bodies

6. These pointed-nosed bugs are the quiet ones. They can be nosed through grass and other cover, and, being streamlined, they pick up and cast nicely.

Sneaky Pete by Gaines.

7. The Spouter, as it is called, is designed to squirt water into the air when it is twitched sharply.

Spouter by Bill Gallasch. This unusual bug was designed to squirt water into the air on the retrieve.

8. Any long, slim body is easier to cast than a squatty body with an equal mass. But this design doesn't have as much face surface as 1, 2, or 3 and therefore won't make as much fuss. The long, slim shape can, of course, be used for pushers and sliders as well as poppers.

9. Most flat-bottomed bugs pick up much easier than bugs with rounded bottoms. I prefer flat-bottomed bugs, but they are seldom available commercially because they can't be shaped with rotary cutting tools. These bugs are easy for the craftsman to form, however, as shown in the photograph on page 31.

10. Bugs with flat bottoms and flat tops are easy to cast because of reduced weight and wind resistance, and because they pick up nicely. I often make balsa bugs in this shape.

Balsa bug by the author. The flat bottom and flat top make it comparatively easy to pick up and cast.

Some of the best surface lures for spinning and baitcasting have spinners on them. The fly-rodder can easily devise bug spinners by running a wire through cork or balsa bodies and then adding hardware on either end. Note that there is a bead on the shaft between the spinner blade and the bug's body. This bead provides a bearing surface, permitting the blade to turn freely. Netcraft, Herter's, and other supply houses market all sorts of hardware for making spinner lures—you can even purchase wire-forming tools. The bug shown here is marketed by Marathon Tackle Company. It is a bit heavy for fly-fishing, but do-it-yourselfers can reduce the weight by using a balsa body and a single hook instead of a treble.

3

Dressing the Bug

CORK AND BALSA BUGS are normally dressed with feather tail wings tied in to flare out to either side. And, invariably, a hackle collar is wound on between the tail and the bug's body. As a rule, the tail wings should be about 1½ times the length of the bug's body—but I break this rule more often than not.

I prefer long, slim neck feathers for bass bug wings, but the less expensive saddle feathers work very well. Fortunately, large feathers are easy to obtain as compared to top-quality dry-fly hackle. The best bet is to purchase a whole neck from a good supply house so that you can select matching wing feathers from either side. Usually, two or three matched pairs of feathers are used, and they are tied in on either side. The better the feathers match in size and curvature, the neater your bug will be.

You can also purchase neck or saddle feathers in small packets or by the ounce. If you buy packaged feathers, some of them will probably be bent out of shape. These can usually be straightened out by steaming them over boiling water and then letting them dry on a flat surface. A blower-type hair dryer does a nice job.

It's best to store feathers in a tight container—or else treat them heavily with mothballs. This is especially true if you buy an expensive grizzly neck.

The techniques used to tie in feather dressings are illustrated in the photographs that follow. Note that bass bugs can also be dressed with bucktail and other suitable hair. A bunch of squirrel tail tied in behind the bug's body will catch lots of bass, but fishermen usually want something more fancy. Long, streamlined hair tails (such as used on the Ka-Boom-Boom popper, page 28) are effective, and the V-shaped frog legs are popular. The basic procedure for working with hair is covered in Part Three and can easily be adapted to cork or balsa bugs.

Painting the body of the bug doesn't cause me many problems because I simply don't believe that color makes too much difference in a surface lure. But I won't argue the point here. Some bass anglers are crazy on the subject and will carefully select a bug with a beautifully painted frog pattern on top—and a plain yellow bottom!

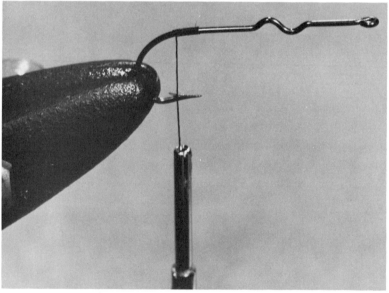

Wrap a hump-shanked hook as shown here and let the thread hang by the weight of the bobbin.

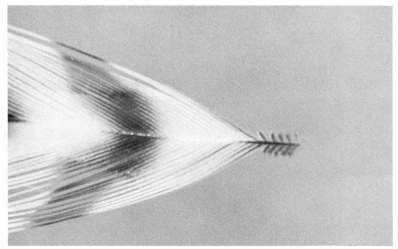

Select four (or six) matching feathers, cut to suitable length, and trim as shown. Trimming the ends in this manner helps prevent the feathers from pulling out.

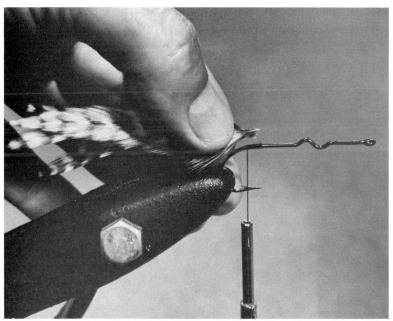

Match the feathers up and hold so that a set flares out to either side.

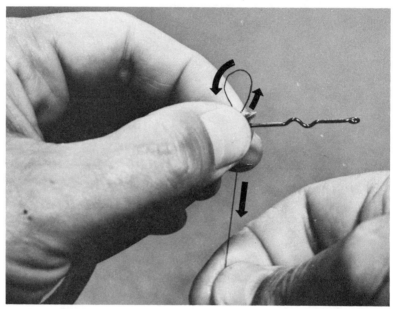

Hold the feathers very firmly. Bring the thread up between thumb and feathers, then loop over and bring down between finger and feathers. Now tighten the thread while holding feathers firm. Repeat for four or five loops. The idea is to hold the feathers and tie them in, directly atop the hook. If you don't hold them firmly, they will tend to rotate around the hook as you tighten the thread down. (See also p. 96.)

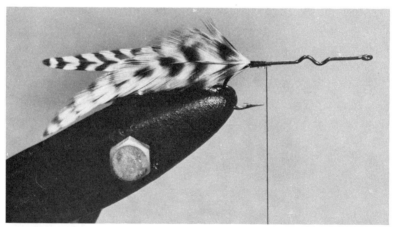

Wrap the ends and apply a drop of head cement.

Select two matching hackle feathers, trim, and tie in as shown here. Before wrapping the ends, however, back the hackles out a bit to provide some clearance, as shown in the next photo; this will make it a little easier to wrap the hackle.

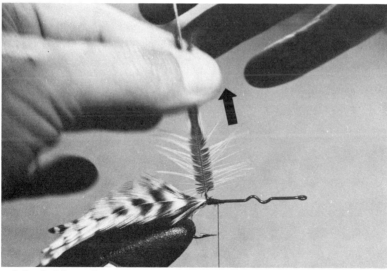

While holding the stems taut with your right hand, moisten your thumb and finger and ruff the hackles out. This will make the fibers stand out better.

Holding the stems firmly, wrap the feathers around the hook so that the fibers stand out. Note: Hackle wrapped in this manner is called dry-fly hackle, which I prefer on bass bugs. Others prefer wet-fly hackle, as shown in the photograph on page 52.

Secure the ends and clip off.

Wrap the thread forward and apply head cement to the windings.

Glue on a slotted cork or balsa body. (Painting the body is covered next in this chapter.)

If you want to apply side dressing to a bug, proceed by sawing or cutting a shallow slot on either side. Fill the slot with a good glue.

Select two matched saddle or neck feathers, align them, hold them directly over the slot, and squeeze them into the slot by applying pressure evenly from both ends. When the feathers are inserted into the slot, the fibers will fold and stick straight out.

After the glue has set, trim the feather stems. (If you want to duplicate this bug, use black and white hackles.)

Balsa bugs should always be painted lest they become waterlogged, but cork bugs don't require any paint at all because the material doesn't absorb water too badly. But most of us paint our bugs whether they need it or not, and the paint does make for a stronger body. Balsa especially needs this added strength.

I normally coat cork with a sealer before painting it, but this isn't necessary. If you want a very smooth body, however, you should fill in the pits with plastic wood (or some such material) and smooth it down with sandpaper before painting. And balsa should be treated with at least one coat of sealer.

I use a ¼-inch hair brush to paint bugs, though bugs can also be dipped in paint or sprayed. Dipping makes for a smooth finish—but it leaves the bug with a clogged hook eyelet. I like a clean eyelet and find it irritating to have to ream the paint out. The smooth finish just isn't that important to me. If you want to try dipping bugs, remember that it's best to thin your paint pretty well so that it will drip off and won't accumulate heavily on the face of the bug when you hang it up to dry.

If you want to turn out really professional-looking bugs, you'll need an artist's airbrush. This is nothing more than a small, precision paint sprayer. An airbrush permits delicate shading from one area to another, which is difficult to achieve with a brush. An airbrush is also used for special effects, such as spraying paint over a netting to produce scale finishes, as on the

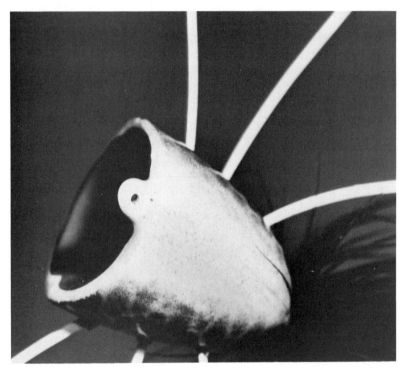

If you dip or spray bug bodies, be certain to get all the paint out of the eyelet. Some commercial bugs have holes drilled or punched through the paint; this may leave sharp edges that can either cut your leader or severely abrade it while you are drawing down the knot.

bug shown in the photograph on page 57. (Such netting is available from Herter's and possibly other supply houses.)

Pressurized spray cans can also be used, but they can't be adjusted like airbrushes. They will do a pretty good job on solid colors, if you aren't fussy about getting paint on the hook's eyelet—and possibly on the hackle and tail feathers.

Actually, your choice of painting methods should depend in large measure on whether you paint the bug's body before or after you have tied in the dressing. This in turn depends on whether you dress the hook before or after it has been glued into the bug's body. I usually dress the hook first. This way, the wrapping thread can be encased in the body instead of having to be tied off against an already painted body. Most commercial bugs, I might add, are tied off after the body has been glued onto the hook, and very frequently the hackle comes loose on these bugs. I also feel that applying rubber legs, as discussed in chapter 1, should be done before the paint job. All this makes it difficult to dip the body in paint, and it limits the use of an airbrush or spray can. I therefore do most of my painting with a brush.

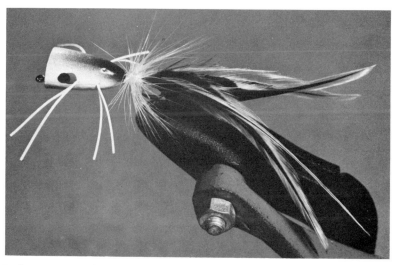

Badger Popper by J. M. Stott. Note the shading from one area to another. Such work is usually accomplished with an airbrush.

Anyhow, any good exterior enamel can be used to paint bugs. The epoxies will probably make a bug stronger, but my personal choice is a flexible enamel sold by Lure-Craft and possibly other sources. This paint is not perfect, but in my experience it doesn't crack and chip as easily as other finishes. Flexible enamel takes a needle nicely and is therefore ideal if you want to thread rubber hackle through the bug's body after the paint job.

Stripes can be made by using masking tape. See the bug on page 18. Eyes and dots can be made on a bug's body with nail heads or dowel pins of suitable size. The trick, of course, is to dip the nail lightly into the paint and then touch it to the bug's body wherever you think the eye or dot should go. Using two such objects of different size permits you to make "pupils" within eyes or small dots within large dots.

Balsa Popper by Poul Jorgensen. Neat eyes . . . and very nice hackle work.

4

Making Bugs Weedless

A BUG—OR ANY OTHER LURE—that is weedless or snagless will not hook bass as effectively as a nonweedless one. Of course, the complete bassman is going to have some weedless lures at hand, and he'll often use them simply because black bass are fond of lily pads, treetops, grass beds, and other peril-

This wire weed guard, shaped like a hairpin, was inserted through the top of this bug (shown upside down) then bent back toward the hook's point. For best results, use a wire no heavier than you really need. Try wire leader material. This is a Gerbubble Bug tied by Bill Gallasch.

ous places. Even so, bass bugs aren't as heavy as plugs and don't have hooks dangling about everywhere, so that a nonweedless bug, gently worked, can be fished in surprisingly tight places. Accurate casting will help.

Judicious bug selection also helps. For example, a heavy popper with a wide face is likely to tangle in grass stems, whereas a pointed-nose bug might be worked fairly successfully.

But weedless bugs are often called for, and, fortunately, the fly-rodder can use several tricks to make a bug more or less weedless. The photographs that follow illustrate some methods that have worked well for me with cork and balsa bugs. Weedless hair bugs and flies are covered in chapters 6, 7, and 10.

Heavy monofilament "limb hoppers" were inserted into this bug (also upside down), made by the author. Because of hooking problems, this method works best on bugs with long bodies.

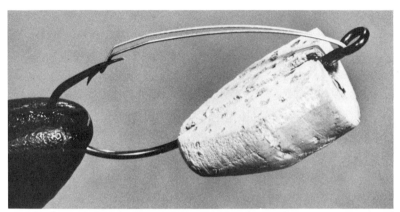

Bug bodies can be glued onto weedless hooks, or, better, similar weed guards can be wrapped onto regular hump-shanked bug hooks. Such weed guards can be bought from some of the supply houses, or you can make your own with light wire.

Flip-up weed guards are used on the weedless Arbogast Hula Popper bugs. If you want to try forming your own, note that the wire curves around the hook's shank from underneath, then loops back through the eyelet.

Monofilament weed guards can be tied onto hump-shanked hooks before you glue on the bug's body. The monofilament is tied in at the tail, then looped over and tied off at the head. More than one strand of monofilament can be used.

Heavy "hackle" can be used as a weed guard. The hackle shown here was formed by the butt ends of bucktail dressing.

This heavy, thick "hackle" was made by spinning deer hair around the hook. The spinning technique will be covered in the next chapter.

If tied densely, regular hackle can make a bug semiweedless. Using stiff hackle and spraying it with Scotchgard will help.

Pad Popper, designed and made by Bill Hutchison. Here's a weedless bug made on a central-draught hook (Mustad 3777). The tail is a combination of bucktail and feathers, but the exact materials aren't too important. What is important is that the point of the hook rides up, and the wing forms a weed guard. It's a good design, and a new one, that has great potential in bass fishing. The head, made of balsa, is constructed as shown in the accompanying drawings, which have been reproduced from the May/June 1976 issue of *Fishing World*. Notice that there is a cavity in the body, which permits the wrappings to be neatly concealed and protected.

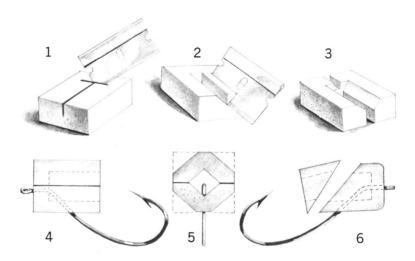

PART TWO

Hair Bugs

Opposite: 1. Make a T-shaped slot in each body block—two blocks per bug. Each block (for a No. 22 central-draught hook) is ¼" x ½" x about ¾" long. 2. Cut a small wedge out of each side of the centerline to provide a V-notch. Do this to both halves for a diamond-shaped cavity to accept the tail. 3. One block (to be the bottom half) is now slotted fore and aft with a small saw to receive the hook. Careful—the V-notch cavity has weakened the block. 4. The hook should fit in the bottom block as shown. Use plenty of glue to secure it; then glue on the top block and let dry overnight. 5. Slice off the corners and sand the body to a smooth diamond shape. 6. The corners on the front of the body are rounded off just slightly, but the aft portion must be cut away as closely as possible to allow clearance so striking fish will come in contact with the point of the hook.

5

Spinning Deer Hair

ACCORDING TO A FRIEND OF MINE, a large foods company sent free samples of a new breakfast cereal to some children located around the country. In addition to market research, the idea was to obtain endorsements for the product, and the children were asked to write, in their own words, why they liked the new cereal. One boy wrote that he liked the stuff because it didn't pop and crackle; it just sat there and sogged! Well, this boy could conceivably grow up in quest of jungle cock and other fancy plumage, but I think he has the making of a hair-bug man.

The body hair from deer, elk, and caribou is hollow, and more or less floatable bugs can be made from it. How high a hair bug will float depends on how it is tied, how long it is fished, and whether it is treated with dry-fly dope or line dressing. Although hair bugs simply don't have the bounce of balsa, it is possible to tie a hair bug that floats quite high. And they can even be tied to pop like dished-faced cork bugs! But the way most of us tie them, hair bugs sog instead of pop. They sit low in the water and may even sink.

Both workmanship and design determine how well a hair bug casts. Some of them cast nicely indeed. In general, soggy hair bugs are heavy and are difficult to throw, whereas dry,

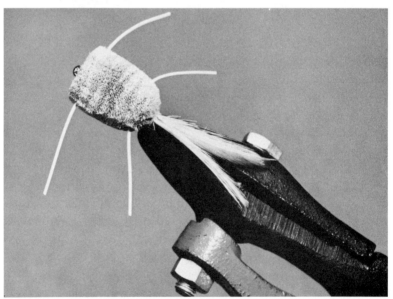

The top bug, from Fly Fisherman's Bookcase, is tied loose and bushy, whereas the bottom bug, from Thomas & Thomas, is dense and trim. Both designs have advantages and disadvantages.

bushy ones are likely to be highly wind resistant. A good deal depends on how tightly the hair is packed onto the hook's shank and on how closely it is trimmed. Some hair bugs are so dense and streamlined that they cast extremely well for their size. But I confess a fondness for loose, bushy bugs. When dry, they are highly wind resistant, but they can be made to light quite gently onto the surface on the cast. After such a bug has soaked up some water, it will sit low and get heavy, almost submerging. On the retrieve, a soggy bug will make quite a wake and, apparently, resembles a mouse or something swimming in the water. Note that rodents, from mice to beaver, as well as frogs and snakes, swim with their body well in the water instead of popping and fluttering about on the surface. In fact, I often fish hair bugs with a slow, steady, wake-making retrieve or with a lunging pull, instead of with sharp, popper-type jerks.

The basic technique for working with hair is illustrated in the following photographs, and design variations are covered in

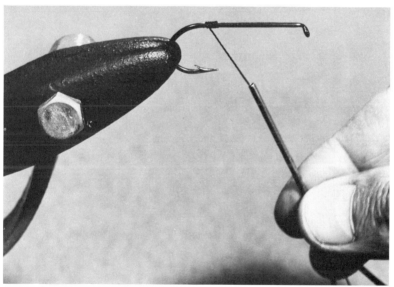

Start a deer-hair bug by winding thread tightly onto the hook's shank near the bend. Do not wrap the entire shank as you would with most flies and streamers. The reason is that the deer hair will spin better on the bare hook shank than it will over a thread wrapping.

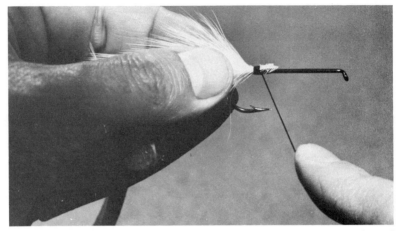

Tie on some sort of tail: in this case, feathers. Trim the butt ends and apply a drop of head cement to the windings.

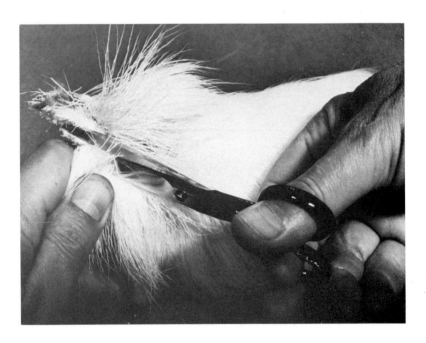

Clip a goodly pinch of hair from a deerskin. When straightened and compressed between the fingers, the bunch should be about the same diameter as an ordinary pencil.

the next chapter. Natural or dyed hair is readily available from most of the supply houses listed in the appendix, and, of course, deer skins may be obtained from hunters. If you order, be certain to list body hair instead of tails. The hair on bucktails, except at the base, is not as buoyant as body hair. Bucktail is, of course, widely used in wings, tails, and so on.

I might add that it is important to have a sturdy vise and strong thread, especially if you want to spin durable, tightly packed hair bugs. I recommend the Thompson F vise and size E nylon thread.

Hold the hair tightly between thumb and forefinger. Place it atop the hook and make two turns with thread. For best results, the finger and thumb should be a little forward of the position shown in the photograph while making the two turns of thread; the thread should be brought up between thumb and hook, then down between finger and hook, so that you can keep a tight grip on the bundle of hair while making the two turns of thread. Then you can back the finger and thumb off a bit, as shown in this photograph. But keep a tight grip on the hair.

Bring the thread straight up, apply pressure with your right hand, and release the hair from left thumb and forefinger. This will spin the hair around the hook. Help the hair over the hook barb with your dubbing needle.

Bunch the hair and pull it back tightly with left thumb and forefinger. Make two turns of thread and a half hitch immediately ahead of the deer hair. Tighten the thread and let hang by the weight of the bobbin. Apply a drop of head cement to the windings.

Cut another bunch of deer hair and spin it around the hook ahead of the first bunch. Note that different colors can be used.

After each application of hair, pack it very tightly to the rear with thumb and forefinger. (A neat hair packer can be made by removing the point and ink well from a ball-point pen.) The tighter you pack the hair, the more dense your bug will be.

When you have spun hair along the entire shank, your bug will look something like this. Take a dozen or so turns of thread at the hook eyelet, then tie off with half hitches or with a whip finish. Saturate the windings with head cement, lacquer, or epoxy. You can fish the bug as it is, but it will be highly wind resistant.

Give the bug a haircut with scissors . . .

. . . and you might end up with a bass catcher like this! With a little practice, you can shape the bug's body most any way you want it, so take a look at the bug patterns illustrated in the next chapter.

6

Designs and Patterns

I HAD THE PRIVILEGE not long ago of sitting in on a discussion with Lew Childre, some of his associates, and a French hook manufacturer. The Frenchman had shown us some purely exquisite dry flies, tied on No. 18 and 22 hooks, which, he thought, might be good for grayling. Quickly, however, the conversation turned to bass and hardware, which, Lew said, was more significant to the hook business. The average bassman, Lew said, had several hundred dollars' worth of plugs and lures, some of which had treble hooks dangling all over them. He asked for a tackle box to illustrate his point.

As it happened, I had a huge box containing about $1,500 worth of lures that I had arranged for a color photograph.

When I opened it up, spreading the trays out fully three feet, the Frenchman gasped. "My God," he said picking up a goggle-eyed Rabble Rouser. "My God," he said, picking up a banana-shaped Lazy Ike. In short, he was simply flabbergasted.

Well, the guy should have seen my bug box. I confess to fishing with outlandish hair bugs that, as Jason Lucas said of the Flatfish, don't resemble anything a bass has ever seen—or hasn't seen. The bass will sometimes hit just about anything that moves, in, on, or over the water. For this reason the creative flytier can really let go when making bass bugs, and deer-hair bodies offer him great range. When used with various tails and wings, hair can be fashioned into a likeness of moths, frogs, and other creatures. Even birds. And natural deer hair properly spun and trimmed, and dressed with whiskers, tail, and eyes, can look enough like a mouse to fool even a smart cat.

The following photographs will give you some ideas. Tie a few, then create your own.

Hair Mouse from Orvis. The ears on this one are made by gluing spun deer hair and then shaping it with scissors. The eyes are painted on, and the tail is a strip of leather.

Tiger Mouse by J. M. Stott.

Large hair moth by Poul Jorgensen. The tail on this one is made from bucktail and flared hackles.

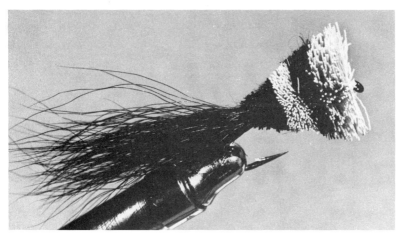

Hair bug designed by H. G. Tapply and made by Dan Bailey's. This bug is clipped flat on the bottom and has a large, burble-making face. It's a great design.

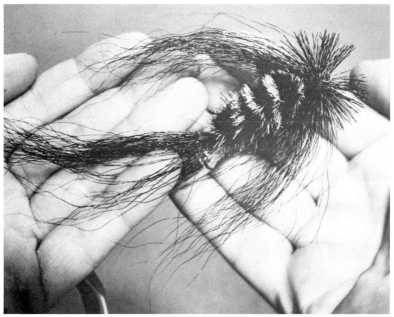

The author is fond of making and fishing with large, ungodly bugs like this, especially when he is in lunker largemouth country. Favorite colors are black and yellow.

This long, slim bug by the author has a peacock herl tail.

Mug-Zee Frog from Raymond C. Rumpf & Son.

Hair frog by Poul Jorgensen. The bucktail legs on this bug are shaped, and held in shape, by thin pieces of copper wire. The wire is inserted at the bend of the leg, then wrapped in with thread. Most of the bent-leg frogs are made in this manner. *Note:* It is important that bucktail legs not be too stiff. The legs should bend back when the frog is moved in the water. Very stiff legs will also cause you to miss some strikes.

Froggie Doggie from Fly Fisherman's Bookcase. The eyes on this one are made from plastic beads, strung up and tied in with thread.

Hair frog by J. M. Stott.

Flat hair bug by Ted Godfrey. Trimmed flat on top and bottom, this bug casts nicely indeed for its size. If you want to cast a large-profile bug on a small fly line, this is probably the way to go. The bug shown here is red and white, but other color combinations are also effective.

Jet Bug by Poul Jorgensen. Only the body of this one is made from deer hair. The tail, back, and whiskers are dark moose mane.

Hairy Mary from Gaines. To make this bug, tie in the hair all the way around the hook's shank immediately behind the eyelet. Then fold the hair back to form head and tail, and coat the head with clear lacquer. (If you want to make larger bugs of this type, try elk hair, which is longer than deer body hair.)

Shown upside down, this is a weedless hair bug by the author. The tail
is black bucktail, and the wings are merely unclipped deer body hair.
Note that the deer hair is trimmed out from the hook's bend.

Henshall Bug from H. L. Leonard's. This is an old but still very good pattern originated by an early champion of the black bass, Dr. James Henshall. The tail is made from two red hackles about the length of the bug's body. The feathers flare out. The tail also contains some strands of unclipped deer hair from the bug's body. The body is black and yellow, with part of the center black segment projecting down to form a weed guard. The wings are white bucktail tied in to stand out and up at about a 45-degree angle. (Other colors are also effective.)

Monofilament weed guard on a bug made by the author.

Hair Popper by the author. Many hair bugs can be made into true poppers by forming a dished-out surface on the face. The author often uses several coats of Pliobond glue to form the surface. In this bug, however, flexible black paint was used. Most hair bugs sit lower in the water than cork or balsa bugs, so that a popper has a different action.

Dragon Fly from Dan Bailey's. Body and tail: natural deer hair completely surrounding hook's shank, secured with blue ribbing. Wings: four Plymouth Rock feathers, tied in to represent open wings. Hackle: light brown.

7

Muddlers, Spuddlers, and Miracle Bugs

MADE WITH A HEAD of spun deer hair, the Muddler Minnow is one of the most versatile flies ever devised. The pattern was first tied by Don Gapen during the summer of 1937. According to his son, Dan Gapen, president of Gapen Tackle Company, "It was designed to represent a native minnow called Cockatush, of the Nipigon River watershed, located in northern Ontario. In actuality, they were really sculpins. Dad called it a Muddler because that was the name given to this type of minnow in the area he grew up in—southern Wisconsin." The minnow has a flattened head, tapered body, and big pectoral fins. Gapen tied his imitation with deer hair, gray squirrel tail, mottled turkey wing sections, and flat gold tinsel.

A muddler can be fished on the surface like a bug, or it can be fished wet like a streamer. One method that sometimes produces for me is to play a muddler on the surface awhile, then let it sink slowly to the bottom. Often a strike will come while the lure is sinking. If it hits bottom without a strike, hop it along for several feet.

Although the Muddler was originated for brook trout, it can be quite effective on black bass and other game fish when tied on very large hooks. It looks sort of like a bullhead when fished along the bottom, and I've seen several lunker bass—7- and 8-

pounders—that had bullheads in their gullet. So, be sure to try a large muddler on a fast sinking line. Also try weighted muddlers.

Dan Bailey, Dave Whitlock, and others have modified the original muddler, and some of the variations are covered in the

Original Muddler Minnow as tied by Gapen Tackle Company. Tail: section from mottled brown turkey quill. Body: gold tinsel. Underwing: gray squirrel tail. Wing: matched sections of mottled turkey quill. Collar: brown deer hair. Head: brown deer hair, clipped.

photographs that follow. I have also included in this chapter the weedless Miracle Bug, tied on a Keel hook. This is not a muddler, but it is fairly close because the heads of both types are made of spun deer hair. Anyhow, the Miracle Bug is a great bass catcher; because it is fairly weedless, it can be fished in lily pads, treetops, and similar cover that would snag a regular muddler.

I have also included in this chapter my own all-time favorite deer-hair bass catcher. It is tied on a Keel hook and has a body made primarily from polypropylene yarn. The photographs on pages 88 through 90 show how this bug is put together.

Muddler Minnow from Dan Bailey's. Tail: section of brown speckled turkey quill. Body: gold tinsel. Underwing: white over brown calf's tail. Wing: matched sections of mottled turkey quill. Collar: brown deer hair. Head: spun brown deer hair, trimmed.

Missoulian Spook as tied by Dan Bailey's. Tail: section of lightly speck-led turkey wing quill. Butt: red chenille. Body: white angora rabbit's wool, ribbed with silver tinsel. Underwing: barred teal flank feather fibers over sparse white calf's tail. Wing: two matched lightly speckled turkey wing quill sections. Collar: brown deer hair. Head: spun white deer hair.

Whitlock Sculpin (originated by Dave Whitlock) as tied by Dick Su-rette's. Body: creamish-yellow blend of seal fur and orlon (or substitute) ribbed with oval gold tinsel. Underwing: red fox squirrel tail. Wing: two barred cree neck hackles, tied flat over underwind; topped by mallard or prairie chicken breast feather, also tied in flat. Shoulder: two barred breast feathers from mallard hen or prairie chicken tied in on either side at the base of the wing; each feather should flare out slightly. Collar: deer hair, light on bottom, darker on top. Head: light, yellowish deer hair, clipped wide and flat.

Black Marabou Muddler from Dan Bailey's. This one is the same as the White Marabou Muddler except that it has black wings and a white underwing. Other colors can also be used.

White Marabou Muddler from Dan Bailey's. Tail: sparse bunch of red hackle fibers. Body: tinsel chenille. Underwing: tan calf's tail. Wing: two matched turkey marabou feathers tied in to flare out slightly to either side. Wing is topped with 10 or 12 peacock herls. Collar: deer hair. Head: spun deer hair, trimmed.

Spuddler originated by Don Williams and Red Monical, as tied by Dan Bailey's. This one is a cross between a muddler and a dark spruce streamer. Tail: very short bunch of brown hair. Body: yellow angora rabbit wool or substitute, with a patch of red wool immediately behind the head. Collar: red fox squirrel tail tied in on the sides and top but not on the bottom. Head: brown spun deer hair trimmed flat and rather wide. The bottom is trimmed almost flush with the body.

Miracle Bug by Keel Fly Company. This bass catcher has a Muddler-like head tied on a Keel hook. Tail: matched pairs of saddle or neck feathers. Body: deer body hair secured to the hook's shank with heavy thread. Wing: deer body hair. Head: deer body hair.

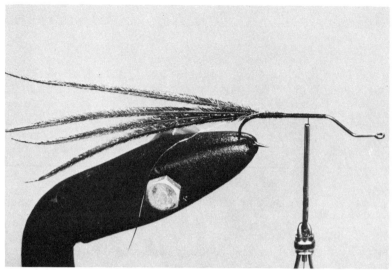

The author's favorite bass bug is started by wrapping the shank of a Keel hook from the offset back to the bend. Tie in a bunch of peacock herl. Also tie in a strand of embossed silver (or gold) tinsel. Then wrap the thread forward.

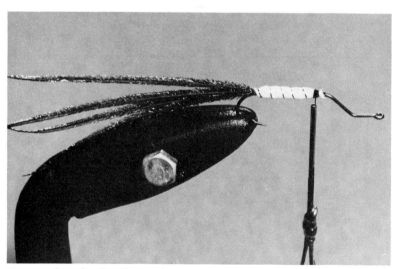

Tie in a length of yellow polypropylene yarn. Wrap yarn back to tail. Then bring it forward and secure with a turn or two of thread. Next, wrap the tinsel forward and secure. Add a drop of head cement.

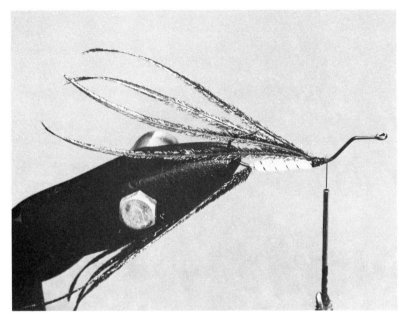

Tie in another bunch of peacock herl.

Spin black deer hair up the bend and to the hook eyelet.

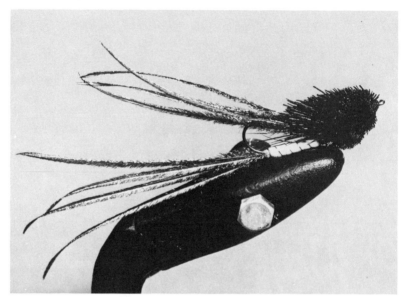

Trim the deer hair pretty much as shown here. Note that the point of the hook will ride up, and that the deer hair forms a weed guard.

PART THREE

Streamers, Bucktails, and Flies

8

Easy Streamers
and Bucktails

WITH FEW EXCEPTIONS, both streamers and bucktails
are intended to imitate minnows and baitfish. The one difference between the two is that bucktails are dressed only with
bucktail or similar hair, whereas streamers are dressed primarily
with feathers, although they may contain some hair and other
materials.

The easiest way to make streamers is to form a head with
epoxy putty and embed some hackles in it. The hackles should
be trimmed as shown in the photograph on page 43, and the
epoxy head should be applied near the eye of the hook. A disad-
vantage of these streamers is that epoxy heads are heavy. But
there are advantages. The hackles can be placed nicely, and the
epoxy head takes a paint job beautifully. The biggest advantage
is that the relatively heavy epoxy head gives the streamer an up-
and-down jiglike motion on the retrieve. (This same effect can
be achieved by wrapping lead wire around the head of conventional streamers.) If you want to make some epoxy streamers, be
sure to try one with long, slim neck hackles and bump it along
the bottom.

The next two photographs show epoxy-head streamers, and
the rest of the photographs in this chapter illustrate how simple
bucktails and streamers can be made with conventional materials.

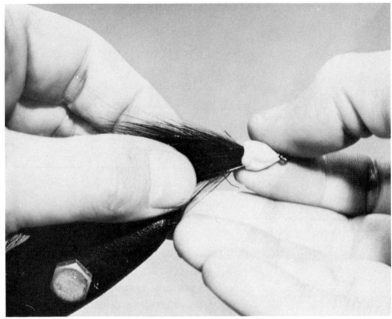

Start epoxy-head streamers by roughly shaping a head with properly mixed epoxy putty. Then select four matching saddle or neck feathers, trim the butt ends, and insert them into the epoxy. Let dry thoroughly.

After the epoxy material has dried, sand the head down smoothly and paint it.

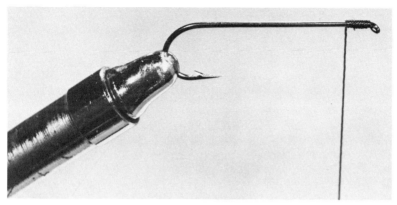

To begin a simple streamer, wrap the hook's shank from the eyelet back. Wrap it tightly, and apply a drop of head cement. (The thread, of course, is wrapped over itself: then the tag end is trimmed.)

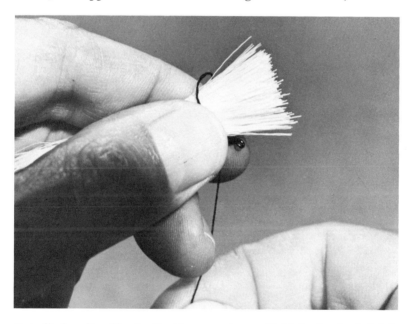

Cut off a bundle of bucktail with your scissors. Hold the bucktail tightly between thumb and forefinger atop the hook. Bring the thread up between thumb and bucktail, loop it over, and bring it down between forefinger and bucktail. At this point, you should have a loop in the thread. Hold everything tightly while slowly pulling down on the thread. Snug the bucktail down, but don't apply too much pressure.

Still holding the bucktail tightly atop the hook, take several more turns of thread. Then release the bucktail and let the thread hang by the bobbin. Apply a drop of head cement. If you'll look closely at this photograph, you'll see that the bucktail tends to rotate on the hook's shank as you apply pressure on the thread. To hold this rotation to a minimum, you must hold the bundle tightly.

Trim the ends of the bucktail at an angle so that the fly head will slope down toward the eyelet. This will prevent a bulky buildup of material.

Build up the head with thread, then tie off with a whip finish (discussed in the last caption in this chapter). Then apply several drops of
head cement and let it dry. Note that the head on this bucktail is
pretty rough. That is because a very large thread was used. Compare
this to the head on the streamer in the next chapter (page 104), which
was tied with nymph thread.

Note that two or more colors of bucktail can be used, and that eyes can
easily be painted on the head.

To make easy streamers, wrap on two or three pairs of matching neck or saddle feathers. The feathers should be selected and trimmed just as they are in making bass bug wings (chapter 3), but the feathers should curve inward on streamers instead of flaring out as on bass bugs. (A few streamer patterns, however, are tied feather-duster style.)

The simple streamer will catch bass, but notice the improvement made (at least in appearance) merely by adding an imitation jungle-cock eye! More fancy dressings are covered in the next chapter.

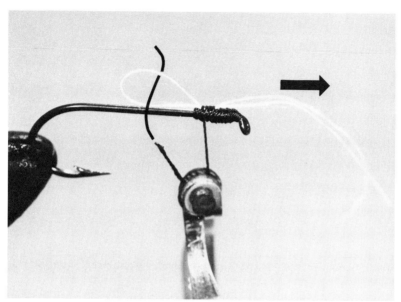

The heads on streamers and bucktails can be tied off with simple half hitches, but a whip finish is better. You can use one of the whip-finish tools available from the supply houses, or you might puzzle out a manual whip-finish method. But I'll tell you what *I* do, although Poul Jorgensen, Dave Whitlock, and some of the other sharps might ruffle their hackles a bit. I use the rod maker's tie-off method, as illustrated in the photograph. A short piece of thread is doubled and held atop the fly head so that a loop is formed in one end. This short piece (white) is wrapped several times with the head thread (black). The tag end of the black thread is then inserted into the loop. The ends of the white thread are grasped and pulled as indicated by the arrow. This brings the tag end of the wrapping thread back under itself. After the surplus has been pulled through and the thread snugged tight, the tag end is trimmed off. Then head cement or lacquer is applied with a bodkin.

9

Dressing a Fly

FANCY STREAMERS, bucktails, and wet flies are usually dressed more or less according to standard patterns. Materials may vary quite a lot, but tails, wings, and hackle are usually tied in pretty much the same way from one pattern to another.

Normally, a tail is tied in first. Then a body of some sort is wrapped onto the hook's shank. The wings are tied in last. And you can have cheeks, beards, underwings, and so on. Possibly the best way to illustrate the making of a fly is to photograph one under construction from tail to head. The photographs and captions on pages 101 through 104 show how a version of the badger streamer is made. Tying in various other body materials, such as palmer hackle, is covered in the rest of the photographs.

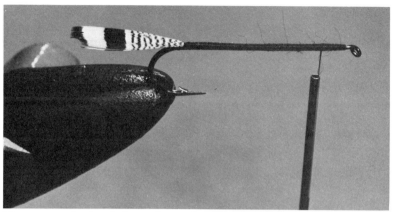

First, wrap the hook from the eyelet back to the bend. Then tie in a tail. (Wood-duck side feathers are used here.) After the tail has been tied in, wrap the thread back toward the eyelet. Leave enough room to tie in wings and other dressings; the exact distance will vary with the size of the hook and the materials required. After tying a few flies, you'll develop a feeling for this, so just remember that beginners usually don't leave enough room to finish off a fly properly.

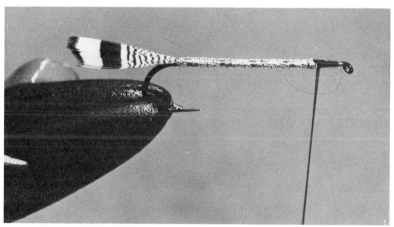

Tie in a strand of embossed tinsel near the eyelet and wrap it back to the base of the tail; then wrap it forward and secure with a few turns of thread. (Your streamer will now look like the photograph.) It is important that you wrap the tinsel tightly and carefully. Avoid overlapping the tinsel, and avoid a buildup at the tail. The turns of tinsel should fit edge to edge so that the whole works won't slip and loosen.

Tie in a sparse underwing of white bucktail.

After taking a few turns around the underwing, trim the ends of the bucktail diagonally toward the eyelet, as shown in this photograph. (Cutting the bucktail at this angle helps form a smooth head later.) Then tie in a sparse beard of white bucktail underneath the hook's shank.

Select two sets of matched badger neck hackles. Trim the butt ends and arrange the hackles so that each set curves in toward the other instead of flaring out as on bass bugs. Hold the hackles firmly and secure with several turns of thread. Let the thread hang by the weight of the bobbin and inspect the hackles. Straighten if necessary and add head cement to the windings.

Next, tie in cheeks on either side. Barred wood-duck side feathers are used here, matching the tail.

Build up the head with thread, tie off with a whip finish (p. 99), and coat with lacquer. Then paint an eye on either side of the head, if the pattern or your fancy calls for eyes. Nymph thread was used to tie this streamer because it ties flat and makes for a smooth head.

Opposite: Mylar, a popular body material for saltwater flies, is also effective on bass flies. Mylar ribbon can be wrapped on like tinsel. Tubing is cut to suitable length and slipped on over the hook eye, as shown in the photograph above. Note that the thread is hanging from the rear of the hook. The end of the Mylar tube is wrapped with thread and tied off with a whip finish. Then the thread is wrapped around the shank near the hook eye and the front end of the tubing is wrapped, as shown in the bottom photograph. Now you're ready to tie in the wings and other dressings.

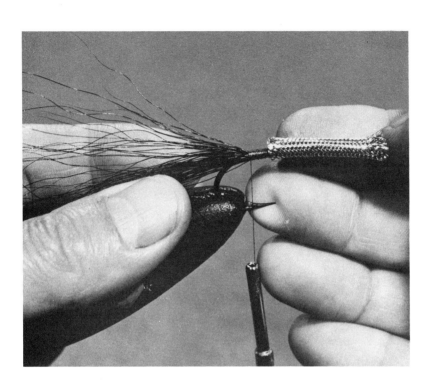

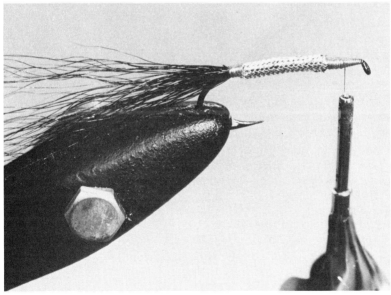

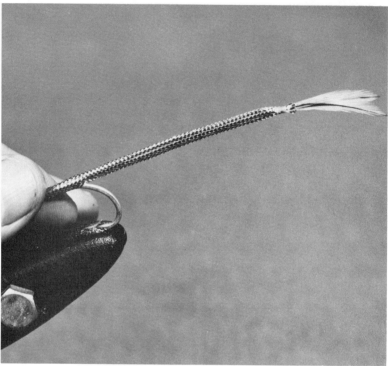

Piping can also be extended to the rear of the hook. The hook's point is inserted into the tube and out through the tubing wall. Then the tubing is secured with thread at the head. Note the teaser tail at the rear of the tubing. Matching feather tips were inserted into the end of the tubing. Then the end was tied off. This photograph was made from a Silver Fancy streamer, designed and tied by Poul Jorgensen. For the complete streamer, see the photograph on page 118.

Chenille and various yarns are popular body materials. Typically, chenille (and similar materials) is tied in at the tail. Then the tying thread
is wrapped forward. The chenille is wound around the hook's shank
and tied off near the head. In the photograph, two strands were tied in
at the tail: the white was wrapped forward and secured with a few
turns of thread; the black strand is being wrapped over the white.
When using two strands, I wrap one clockwise and the other coun-
terclockwise. But the two strands can also be wrapped simultaneously.

The palmer hackle is a very old way of making hairy bodies for various fly patterns. In the Wooly Worm shown here, a strand of chenille and a large hackle were tied in at the tail. The chenille was wrapped forward and secured with a few turns of thread. Then the hackle is wrapped over the chenille in a spiral. (More than one hackle can be tied in.) Try to space the turns so that the butt end of the hackle will end up at the point where your thread is hanging. Then tie off with a whip finish (p. 99).

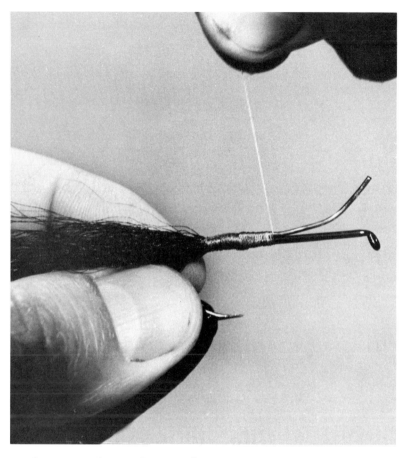

Lead wire can be used to weight flies. Fine wire can be wrapped
around the hook's shank, or larger wire can be wrapped onto the shank
with thread, as shown here. In any case, the lead should be completely
covered with lacquer to prevent it from discoloring fancy dressings.

10

Patterns

BLACK BASS can be quite selective, especially when they are feeding on schooling baitfish. I've seen anglers fishing during such a feeding spree—with bass sloshing water all about the boat—without drawing a single strike. In such cases, the angler should determine what the bass are feeding on and try to match it exactly, especially in length and profile. Often a maimed baitfish can be found kicking on the surface.

But usually bass aren't as selective as trout, and they will often hit any reasonable offering that is presented and fished correctly. Thus, exact patterns aren't usually too terribly important in bass fishing. Even so, the beginning flytier should attempt to duplicate some of the standard patterns for their own sake. A tier is not accomplished until he can do this.

Most of the trout, salmon, and steelhead flies will take bass if they can be tied large enough. To be sure, tiny flies will take bass (especially the little redeye), and I've caught a 7-pound largemouth on a No. 10 nymph—but you will surely do better, day in and day out, with the larger flies, especially if you're in lunker largemouth country. Unfortunately, fly patterns especially for bass have not been developed to any great extent, but, fortunately, many of the standard patterns, especially those designed for salt water, can be tied in large sizes. In many other cases, however, the materials required for a fly preclude its service as a normal bass catcher. It is difficult to tie a large Adams, for example, because quality dry-fly hackle is small, and no way can it be used successfully on a ¹/₀ hook. A Mickey Finn, on the other hand, can be tied quite large because it is dressed with bucktail, which is available in lengths in excess of 4 inches if you purchase extra-large northern tails. Long neck and saddle hackles can also be obtained easily, and it is possible to tie a streamer 7 or 8 inches long.

Many of the standard patterns can be adapted to Keel hooks. Because the point of a Keel hook rides up, the wing dressing can be tied so that it forms a weed guard. The danger here is that too much wing dressing will make it difficult to hook a bass. Feathers and dense bucktail can mat over the hook's point, so be careful. Keel hooks do, however, have great potential in bass flies simply because they can be fished in grass beds, lily pads, treetops, and other tight places.

All of the streamer, bucktail, and fly patterns featured in the following photographs will catch bass. The materials used in each illustrated pattern are specified in the captions, and the proportions of the various materials can be determined from the photographs.

Bass Buddy by J. M. Stott. Body: white floss with silver ribbing, lacquered. Wings: matched pairs of white-over-yellow saddle feathers. Beard: white saddle fibers. Shoulder: red breast feather with junglecock eye. Head: black, lacquered.

Feather Streamer from Dan Bailey's. Tail: two sets of matched feathers, tied in to flare out. Body: very bushy hackle. According to Bailey's, "This is a very useful type fly with more action in the water than other streamers. It is the most effective wet fly for bass we ever used . . . particularly good when used with a small spinner." Colors can vary, but Bailey's offers the following combinations:

Tail	*Hackle*
Red and white	Red and white
Red and grizzly	Red and grizzly
Red and yellow	Red and yellow
Black and orange	Orange and black
Red and blue	Red and blue
Green and brown	Green and brown

Mickey Finn (Hi-Ti style) by Poul Jorgensen. Wings: yellow bucktail tied in bunches from the hook's bend forward, with a bunch of red bucktail under yellow near the head. Body: red thread, well lacquered. Head: red, lacquered, with black-on-white eyes. *Note:* a number of streamer and bucktail patterns can be tied in this style. Typically, the wings of such streamers and bucktails ride high, even when wet.

McNally Magnum as tied by Jim Poulos. Body: yellow chenille. Wings: six large, long, yellow saddle feathers. Hackle: red. Head: black, lacquered. McNally designed this one for northern pike about twenty years ago, but, as he told me, "bass eat them up." The Magnum is a good example of how very large flies can be tied for bass; in fact, the one shown here is a little over 6 inches long.

Tarpon Rooster by J. M. Stott. Tail: two matched sets of yellow saddle feathers, flared out as on bass bugs. Body: silver Mylar tube, tied off at rear with white nylon thread. Wings: two yellow saddle feathers, curved up and out. Hackle: yellow. Head: yellow fluorescent floss with bead-chain eyes tied in by cross-whipping, lacquered.

Fuller Pattern by J. M. Stott. Body: white floss ribbed with silver tinsel. Wings: two red and two yellow saddle feathers, with yellow on inside. Shoulder: natural black saddle hackle tied in on either side with cheeks of peacock saddle tips. Beard: red saddle fibers, sparse. Head: fluorescent yellow floss with gold bead-chain eyes tied in by cross-whipping, lacquered.

Sands Bonefish Fly (originated by Hagen Sands) from Thomas & Thomas. No tail or body. Wing: white bucktail under matched pairs of grizzly over yellow hackle feathers. Head: black, lacquered.

Platinum Blonde (originated by Joe Brooks) as tied by the author. Tail: white bucktail. Body: silver Mylar tinsel. Wing: White bucktail. Head: black, lacquered. There are several other "blond" patterns, including:

Strawberry. Tail: red bucktail. Body: silver Mylar. Wing: orange bucktail.

Honey. Tail: yellow bucktail. Body: gold Mylar. Wing: yellow bucktail.

Mickey Finn. Tail: yellow. Body: silver. Wing: yellow-over-red.

Black. Tail: black. Body: silver. Wing: black.

Argentine. Tail: white. Body: silver. Wing: blue.

Pink. Tail: pink. Body: gold. Wing: pink.

Katydid. Tail: white. Body: silver. Wing: green.

Irish. Tail: light green. Body: silver. Wing: dark green.

Marion Marabou (originated by Chester Marion) as tied by Dan Bailey's. Body: tinsel chenille. Wing: Marabou topped with peacock herl. (As Dan Bailey put it, "These are tied with·various colors of marabou, which are in larger amounts of a predominant color and lesser amounts of other colors for touches.") Cheeks: hen pheasant feathers. Head: black, lacquered.

(Opposite)

Lefty's Deceiver (originated by Lefty Kreh) as tied by H. L. Leonard's. Tail: two pairs of matched white saddle feathers with a strip (or two strips) of silver Mylar tinsel on either side. Body: silver Mylar tinsel. Wings: small bunch of white bucktail atop hook's shank. Throat: small bunch of white bucktail, matching wings. Head: white, lacquered. (Other colors are also used, especially red.)

Gray Ghost Streamer as tied by J. M. Stott. Body: Silver Mylar tubing tied off with white nylon thread. Wings: black and white saddle feathers, two white over one black on either side. Beard: white neck hackle over sparse red saddle fibers. Shoulder: jungle-cock eye (or imitation). Head: black, lacquered.

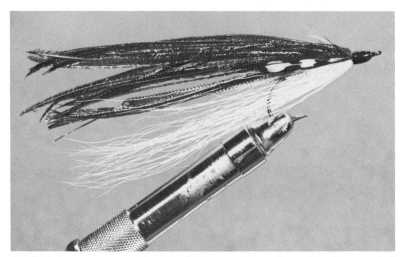

Sand Eel variation tied by Poul Jorgensen. Body and tail: extended Mylar piping (note that the tail is unraveled and tied off). Wing: peacock herl. Throat: white bucktail. Shoulder: jungle cock or substitute. Head: black, lacquered.

Silver Fancy by Poul Jorgensen. Tail: two badger hackle tips tied into extended Mylar tubing. Body: Mylar tubing. Wing: bucktail, dark blue over light blue over white. Shoulder: jungle-cock feather or substitute. Head: black, lacquered.

Needlefish as tied by J. M. Stott. Body: Mylar tube with stiffener insert. Wings: two white saddle feathers over black jungle-fowl saddle feather on each side, topped by peacock fibers. Hackle: white neck hackle. Head: black, lacquered.

Big Hole Demon from Dan Bailey's. Tail: two badger tips. Body: back half, silver tinsel; front half, badger palmer hackle over black chenille.

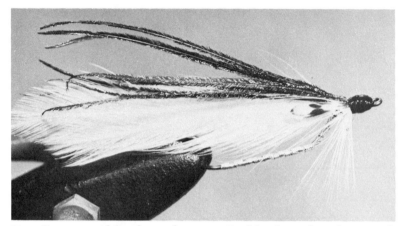

Jane Craig as tied by the author on a Keel hook. Body: silver tinsel. Beard: white saddle hackle (applied before wing). Wing: six white saddle hackles, three on either side, and eight strands of peacock herl on top. Cheek: jungle cock eye or substitute. Head: black, lacquered.

Cockroach as tied on a Keel hook by the author. Tail and body: none. Wing: two matched pairs of long grizzly hackles. Collar: brown bucktail, sparse. Weed guard: two strands of stiff monofilament. Head: black lacquered. *Note:* This fly is a variation of one tied by Lefty Kreh for tarpon. The author ties it on a Keel hook and adds a weed guard, thereby making it suitable for use in very thick grass beds and similar cover.

Fat Fly by Bill Hutchison. Here's a great new fly tied on a Mustad 3777 central-draught hook. Tail: red hackle fibers. Body: white chenille on lower end, lacquered tying thread on upper end. Wings: bucktail (white and black here) tied in small bunches, Hi-Ti style. Head: black, lacquered, with yellow eyes. Materials and colors aren't as important as the basic design, and Hutchison himself, writing in the May–June 1976 issue of *Fishing World*, encouraged readers to experiment with patterns on the central-draught hook. Flies can be tied fuller on this hook, and they have a jiglike motion in the water. Hutchison recommends that you weight these flies a bit.

Green Snook Streamer by J. M. Stott. Body: white floss with silver tinsel ribbing. Wings: matched black, yellow, and green saddle feathers on either side; green on the outside, yellow in the middle, and black on the inside. Beard: a few strands of long red polar-bear hairs. Hackle: yellow neck hackle. Head: black, lacquered.

Royal Coachman Steelhead Fly from Dan Bailey's. Tail: golden pheasant tippet fibers. Butt: green peacock herl. (To make a butt this large, twist three or four strands together.) Body: red floss and peacock herl to match butt. Hackle: brown saddle, tied in before the wing. Wing: white polar bear, bucktail, or calf hair. Head: black, lacquered. Note that this is a wet fly. If you want to tie a Royal Coachman streamer, use a wing made of four matching white neck or saddle feathers trimmed to about 1½ times the length of the hook. Also, many of the Royal Coachman flies and streamers are tied with shorter peacock-herl segments.

(Opposite)

Skunk Steelhead Fly from Dan Bailey's. Tail: red hackle fibers. Body: black chenille ribbed with silver tinsel. Hackle: Black, tied in before the wing. Wing: Polar-bear hair, bucktail, or calf tail, white. Head: black, lacquered. This wet fly is tied on a 1/0 up-eyed Atlantic Salmon hook, which is not necessary or particularly desirable for bass—especially if the fly is to be used with a spinner. The patterns shown here and in the next photograph are merely examples of hundreds of wet-fly patterns that can be tied rather large. Most of them will catch bass.

Black Coachman Streamer as tied by Ted Godfrey. Except for the hook and the wing, the materials are the same as for the preceding fly. Godfrey used a regular streamer hook and a wing much longer than was used in the wet-fly pattern. The original Black Coachman Streamer pattern called for black or dark-brown saddle hackles for the wing, but Godfrey says that black bear hair works well for him. He also told me that the Black Coachman has, for some reason, worked out better than any of the other streamer/bucktail types for smallmouth on the Potomac River, which is fished extensively with a fly rod during the summer months.

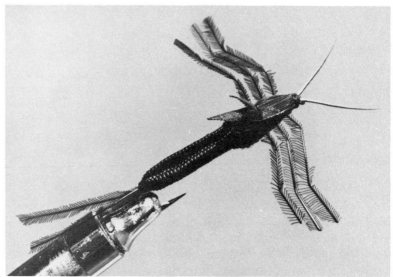

Huge Helgy from H. L. Leonard's. The realistic body on this creation is made from dyed flat cobra monofilament, which is available from some supply houses. The legs on this one are shaped from clipped feathers, and both the top dressings and the antennae were formed from tail- or wing-feather fibers cut to shape. Also try top dressings cut from latex, and antennae made from rubber hackle. For other ideas along this line, see Poul Jorgensen's *Modern Fly Dressings for the Practical Angler*.

Latex nymph by the author. Tail: rubber hackle. Tag: exposed black thread, lacquered. Body: latex. Topknot: deer body hair, calf tail, or similar hair. Head: black, lacquered. Front feelers: rubber hackle.

APPENDIX

Materials

AN OLD POKER BUDDY of mine found out that I had more or less quit that game to pursue the black bass and that, in this pursuit, I had taken up fly-tying. As it happened, he had also quit poker and had taken up cockfighting. He was quite enthusiastic about it and had gotten into such things as the design of steel spurs. "A.D.," he said, "if you're serious about this fly-tying, I can get you all the goddamn rooster feathers you can use!"

I've had similar offers from hunters on deer hides, duck feathers, and so on. Invariably I decline. (I've bought deer tails and things from some supply houses that stank bad enough!) If you want to take advantage of such savings however, I would recommend that you read Eric Leiser's book *Fly Tying Materials: Their Procurement, Use, and Protection.*

Cork and balsa have been covered in Part One of this book, along with hump-shanked hooks. Here are some other materials that are commonly used for bass flies and bugs.

BUCKTAIL. Hair from deer tails is widely used as wings for streamers and as legs, or wings, on bass bugs. Several kinds and grades (length) of bucktail are available, but if you want to tie long streamers it's best to stick with large or extra-large Northern white-tailed deer tails. I always buy extra-large tails and then cut off what I don't need. These large tails are more expensive, however, so that lesser tails might be considered if you tie lots of small or medium-length streamers. The shorter tails can also be used for bass-bug dressings, in which the bug's body contributes to the overall length.

Regardless of length, bucktail is stocked by all the supply houses and is available in natural (white and brown) and in many dyed colors.

Synthetic "hair," such as Dynel, is also available in a variety of colors and in several lengths. This material is certainly satisfactory—and it probably lasts longer than hair—but I personally prefer real bucktail for almost all uses.

OTHER TAILS. Squirrel tail, raccoon tail, calf tail (also called kip or impala), and other tails are additionally used in flies, streamers, and bugs. Most of these are not as long as bucktail and aren't suited for long streamers. Yet some tails, such as large fox squirrel, may have hair as long as 3 inches and can be used for wings and dressing on medium-length streamers and on deer-hair or cork-bodied bass bugs.

All manner of domestic and exotic tails are available from the supply houses, so if ordinary bucktail and a squirrel tail or two don't suit your fancy, write for the catalogs and pore over them.

DEER BODY HAIR. Hair bugs are normally made from deer body hair, which is hollow and light. The length of the hair does vary, but length is not normally specified and isn't often important because the hair is usually clipped to shape.

Deer body hair is widely available from the supply houses, in natural (white and brown) as well as in a variety of colors. It is normally sold by the "piece" (which varies from one supply house to another) or by the square inch. If you tie lots of hair bugs, you might shop around for a whole skin, or half a skin.

OTHER BODY HAIR. The body hair from elk, caribou, and antelope is hollow, like deer body hair, and can be used for spinning floatable bugs. Usually, these are more expensive than deer hair and not often available in a wide choice of colors. But there are some advantages, or differences, as compared to deer body hair:

Antelope hair is coarse and thick, having a gray base and a tan top. It spins nicely and is usually a bit stronger than deer hair. It is an excellent material for making bass bugs.

Caribou hair is light, spins nicely, and flares easily. It is almost the same color as deer hair but is shorter. While it floats better than deer hair, it isn't quite as durable.

Elk hair is from 3 to 4 inches long and is sometimes used for wings on streamers. It is seldom used for bugs, but I (for one) do use it for large hair bugs when I want to leave some hair untrimmed to form wings, tails, whiskers, etc. Elk hair is quite coarse.

Moose mane isn't used for spinning bugs, but it can be used for legs or feelers, and it is called for in the Jet Bug, as shown in the photograph on page 77.

FEATHERS. All manner of feathers—large and small, plain and fancy—are used in tying flies. The most important to the bassman follow.

Hackle feathers that are stiff, nonwebby, and of high quality are hard for the dry-fly purist to find. But the bassman has no big problem except with size, and most of the large supply houses will specify which feathers are large enough for bass bug and streamer wings.

"Hackles" are used not only for wings on streamers and bass bugs, but also for hackle work on cork-bodied bass bugs and on such streamers and flies as the McNally Magnum and the Wooly Worm.

Most of the hackle feathers used for bass work come from roosters and are either neck or saddle hackles. The neck hackles are usually more expensive and can be bought in packets, by the ounce, by the neck, or, sometimes, in matched sets. Generally, the larger the amount, the cheaper they are. But I wouldn't advise the beginner to purchase a whole neck—and I certainly wouldn't advise him to get expensive grizzly or badger hackles until he gains experience. Most of the large streamers and bass bugs shown in the photographs in this book were made with inexpensive, dyed saddle hackles. But see the badger hackles in the photograph on page 104 and the grizzly hackles in the photograph on page 115.

Maribou feathers have great potential in bass streamers—even on bugs—and I feel that I have somewhat neglected them in this book. As the Reed catalog states, "The long soft fibers of these feathers give a very lifelike breathing action in the water. When pulled they draw together and when momentarily stopped they fluff out. For small streamers strip fibers from the quill and tie on same as you would a hair. For larger streamers bunch tip together and cut off, then strip off smaller side fibers and add to bunch." It is great stuff, and is widely available in a variety of colors. See the maribou in the photographs on pages 86 and 116.

Fancy feathers are used in cheeks, underwings, and so on. Often these are feathers from the body of wood ducks, pheasants, and other fowl. Read up on all these in the catalogs—but go slow when ordering. I purchased a bunch of fancy feathers—some of which were quite expensive—when I first started tying flies, and some of them have never been used at all. My best advice is to purchase only the feathers you will need to tie a particular pattern. And keep your repertoire reasonable, unless, of course, the expense of the thing doesn't matter much.

Jungle-cock "eyes" are frequently called for on streamers and flies, but they are becoming more and more difficult to obtain and, of course, more and more expensive. I use the plastic imitations, or else I substitute some other feather. Note that "eyes" and other markings can be painted onto less expensive and readily available feathers.

Peacock herl is used as a secondary wing material in some

streamer patterns, and I am fond of using half a dozen herls as a "tail" on hair bugs. Peacock herls have an almost metallic cast, as reflected in the photograph on page 90.

BODY MATERIALS. A number of materials are used in the bodies of streamers, bucktails, and flies. Some are primarily construction materials used to build up the body; others are added for flash, color, or flair. A good many tiny flies and nymphs have bodies of fur or synthetic material dubbed on thread and wrapped around the hook's shank. Large bass-size streamers and flies, however, are seldom made by this method, so that suitable dubbing materials, such as English hare's ears, are omitted from the following list.

Chenille, a widely used body material, is easy to work with and is used on the famous Wooly Worm and other patterns. It is available in fine, medium, and large sizes. I like the large chenille, but the medium is fine for bass flies. In all sizes, chenille can be purchased in a variety of colors—even variegated. Tinsel and Mylar chenille can also be purchased, and these are great fish attractors. Chenille of all types is usually sold on cards, but larger skeins and assortments are usually cheaper per foot.

Yarn of all kinds can be used in tying flies, and I confess to having scrounged about in my wife's crewel basket. Wool yarn has been used for fly bodies for a long time, and is still quite popular. It soaks up water, and is especially good for streamers. Polypropylene yarn has potential for Muddler-type "floating streamers" and bugs. It has a specific gravity of .96 and floats better than wool, chenille, and other similar body materials.

Floss, made of rayon, acetate, and other materials, ties flat and can be used to build up beautiful tapered bodies. It is available in all manner of colors, usually on spools.

Latex, in sheets which can be cut into strips, is becoming increasingly popular for trout nymphs. It also has great potential for bass-sized, nymphlike lures, as shown in the photograph on page 124. "Heavy duty" latex is usually available in cream color, and thinner latex is available in either cream or charcoal. The cream latex can be colored with permanent felt-tip pens. Note also that cream latex will take on the color of whatever is under it, so that you may want to wrap the hook's shank with bright-colored thread.

Flat monofilament is being used to tie nymphs for trout and has potential in deep-sinking bass lures. Large nymphs and other lures made primarily from flat monofilament, however, are quite heavy.

Tinsel is used as a construction material or as a ribbing wound on over other body materials to add flash to flies and streamers. It is available in gold and silver, and in several widths. Embossed and oval tinsels are also available and popular. I prefer wide tinsels for bass flies, but the medium widths are usually satisfactory.

Mylar, available in sheets, in strips, and in braided piping, is very popular with saltwater fly-rodders. (See the photographs on pages 105, 106, and 114.) The material comes in several sizes of silver and gold piping, and in strips of various widths. Mylar sheets can be cut to the desired widths and come, conveniently with gold on one side and silver on the other.

The Mylar piping comes with a cotton core which is normally removed if a segment of the piping is to be slipped on over the hook's shank. Note also that Mylar piping can also be wound onto the hook's shank. The core is usually removed, but leaving it in will produce a fatter body.

Fine round *wire,* in gold and silver, is sometimes used to add flash and to strengthen the body. For maximum protection, it should be wrapped in the opposite direction of the body material.

Lead wire is seldom used as a dressing; it is used to weight a fly or streamer. It is available in several diameters, and something in the medium range is usually about right for bass flies and streamers.

THREAD. Fly-tying and rod-wrapping thread is available from the supply houses in several sizes, from 18/0 (very, very small) up through E (large). Size E is recommended for spinning large hair bugs because strength is required. Sizes C and D are also good, especially for medium-sized bugs, but they are not available from some supply houses. Size A or 00 will do for most other bass-bug and fly work, although the "flat-tying" nymph thread will produce a very smooth head.

Some dry-fly and nymph sharps—and some professionals—insist on silk thread on the grounds that it has less stretch and therefore won't loosen. True. The problem with silk is that it isn't as durable as nylon, isn't as strong, and costs twice as much.

Most threads are available in several colors. Get whatever you need, but remember that you will probably use black more than any other color.

WAX. My guess is that most flytiers start off using wax on their thread (or buy prewaxed thread) and then drop the practice. I am one of these. I use nylon thread and lots of head cement, so that rotting is not a problem with my flies. Wax does, however, make things a little easier and does help bind the thread to the hook's shank. Wax is also needed if you do much dubbing.

HEAD CEMENT. All the supply houses carry head cement and thinner, and all I've tried has been satisfactory, but more and more I lean toward the quick-drying kinds.

HOOKS. Most of the catalogs specify hooks as dry fly, streamer, wet fly, bass bug, and so on, and these recommendations are usually about right. For this reason, I think the beginner should stay pretty much with hooks purchased from the supply houses. After he becomes familiar with fly hooks and knows what he needs or wants, he should also try regular tackle outlets.

Remember that hooks range from very short to very long, as follows: 5X short . . . 1X short . . . 1X long . . . 8X long. (If a certain hook doesn't have an "X" rating either way, it is the normal hook in its pattern—or else the X was omitted from the specifications.) If this is confusing, don't worry much about it. You'll seldom need short hooks in bass work, and many of the catalogs have actual-size illustrations along with the long hooks. Most of the wet-fly, nymph, and hair-bug hooks range from normal to about 2X long. Most of the streamer and bucktail hooks are 3X long and longer—although it is entirely permissible to tie *some* streamers or bucktails on short hooks. It's a matter of pattern and proportion—a matter of the eye—how a certain pattern *looks* on a certain length hook.

The diameter of the wire in a hook is also specified (or can be specified) by "X" ratings ranging from 2X fine to 4X stout. Is some catalogs, these ratings are not used, but rather such terms as "light wire" and "heavy wire," or "extra heavy wire."

Generally, it is best, by far, to avoid heavy hooks for bass. The larger the hook and the heavier the wire, the more difficult it is to stick a bass. I also avoid the very light hooks, but they do come in handy when tying some bugs and flies. Muddlers, for example, will float better (if you want them to float) when they are tied on a light hook.

Hooks are not cheaper by the dozen. They're cheaper by the hundred and by the thousand. But unless you know exactly what you want, in shape and size, and can specify the hook by number, it's best to get only a dozen of a particular size and kind. I've bought several thousands of hooks that I didn't need—and probably won't ever use.

Whatever hook you choose, remember that very few of them are sharp. Or sharp enough. I always sharpen a new hook if it's size 4 or larger, and I sharpen it again after fishing with it for a while.

Most of the hooks sold for wet or dry flies and for streamers have their eyelet turned up or down. I buy these and use them, but the bassman can get by with regular ringed hooks. This is especially true if he intends to use a spinner attachment ahead of the fly or streamer. A few hooks are made with large eyelets, and spinner attachments work well with these. (Spinner arms tend to bind and foul in small eyelets, doglegging spinner and fly.)

If you can find them, try the British-made hooks. These are expensive, but some of them are truly great.

Tools

ONE OF THE WORST INVESTMENTS I ever made was in cheap fly-tying tools. They were not merely a waste of money, either. Quality tools help you tie quality flies and add to the pleasure of fly-tying—which is difficult to measure in terms of dollars and cents. I haven't tried every tool on the market, and I'm especially lacking in experience with the French and British tools, but in general the adage "you get what you pay for" holds in fly-tying tools. Skimp on materials if you must, but get good tools. Here's what you'll need:

VISE. It is very important that you have a steadfast vise for all fly-tying, and especially in spinning deer-hair bugs. I prefer vises with lever-operated jaws because they are easier and faster to use, and I also like a vise with height adjustments and a rotatable collet. The Thompson A vise has become the standard in vises of this sort, and I recommend it. I use the A even for holding hooks as large as 1/0. The exception is when I am spinning deer-hair bugs, where considerable pressure is required. For spinning hair, I prefer the Thompson F vise, or something similar. The F vise, however, isn't as adjustable or as nice as the A and I use it only reluctantly. People who tie bass bugs and

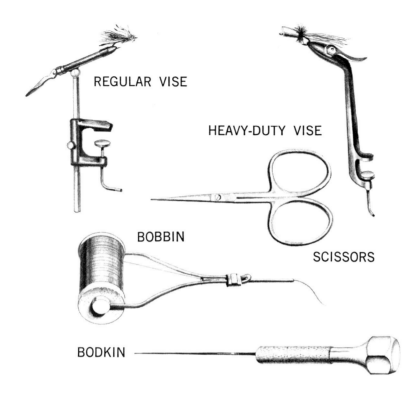

REGULAR VISE

HEAVY-DUTY VISE

BOBBIN

SCISSORS

BODKIN

Tools for tying bugs and flies.

saltwater flies really need a new heavy-duty vise comparable to the A.

Anyhow, get a good vise. It's true that you can tie flies with vise grips, small table vises, and Mickey Mouse clothespin rigs—but for constant and enjoyable and dependable use, nothing beats a good fly-tying vise.

BOBBIN. A bobbin isn't entirely necessary, but I use one 99 percent of the time. The main use of a bobbin, as I see it, is not as a thread-wrapping tool per se; rather, it provides a weight to hold the thread taut while you prepare for the next step in the tying process.

There are several kinds of bobbins of various manufacture. I am not entirely satisfied with any bobbin I've ever used, but if I had to recommend one it would be a simple spring-tension open-frame kind instead of one with screw-mechanism tension controls. But I haven't used all the bobbins, and more and more I'm thinking of going to an open-sided bobbin that will take either large or small spools.

SCISSORS. Good, sharp scissors are mighty nice if you can find them. Surgical scissors are probably best, but they're expensive. I've used manicure scissors, but scissors with larger loops on the handles are easier to work with.

HACKLE PLIERS. These are handy for winding hackles, but I could get by without them for bass bugs and large streamers.

WHIP FINISHER. I purchased one of these that wouldn't work properly for me because it was too limber to tie the thread off tightly. But most whip finishers on the market do a good job, if you like to use them. Instructions are provided—and should be read closely.

HALF-HITCH TOOL. This simple device comes in handy if you want to tie off a head with half hitches. I normally use a whip finish, but half hitches are easier for tying off tightly packed hair bugs and for flies with hackles close up front.

BODKIN. This tool is used primarily for applying head cement and lacquer, but it comes in handy for other purposes. You'll reach for a bodkin often, so get two.

Sources of Tools and Materials

American Anglers
P.O. Box 521
Bethlehem, Pennsylvania 18016

Angler's Mail
6497 Pearl Road
Cleveland, Ohio 44130

Anglers' Nook
P.O. Box 67A
Shushan, New York 12873

Anglers Pro Shop
P.O. Box 35
Springfield, Ohio 45501

Dan Bailey Flies and Tackle
P.O. Box 1019
Livingston, Montana 59047

Bloss Flies
137 Maple Hill Road
Blossburg, Pennsylvania 16912

Bodmer's Fly Shop, Inc.
2400 Naegele Road
Colorado Springs, Colorado 80904

Cascade Tackle Company
2425 Diamond Lake Boulevard
Roseburg, Oregon 97470

Finnysports
2910 Glanzman Road
Toledo, Ohio 43614

Fireside Angler, Inc.
P.O. Box 823
Melville, New York 11746

The Fly Fisherman's Bookcase
and Tackle Service
Route 9A
Croton-on-Hudson, New York
10520

Gene's Tackle Shop
P.O. Box 7701
Rochester, New York 14622

Hackle & Tackle Company
553 North Salina Street
Syracuse, New York 13208

The Hackle House
4117 Peralta Boulevard
Fremont, California 94536

Herter's
Route 1
Waseca, Minnesota 56903

E. Hille
P.O. Box 269
Williamsport, Pennsylvania 17701

H. L. Leonard Rod Company
25 Cottage Street
Midland Park, New Jersey 07432

Bud Lilly's
P.O. Box 387
West Yellowstone, Montana
  59758

Midland Tackle Company
66 Route 17
Sloatsburg, New York 10974

Netcraft Company
3101 Sylvania Street
Toledo, Ohio 43613

Ojai Fisherman
218 North Encinal Avenue
Ojai, California 93023

The Orvis Company, Inc.
Manchester, Vermont 05254

Rangeley Region Sports Shop
28 Main Street
Rangeley, Maine 04970

Reed Tackle
P.O. Box 390
Caldwell, New Jersey 07006

Hank Roberts Outfitters
P.O. Box 308
Boulder, Colorado 80302

Rod and Reel
P.O. Box 132
Leola, Pennsylvania 17540

Raymond C. Rumpf & Son
P.O. Box 176
Ferndale, Pennsylvania 18921

Streamborn Flies
13055 S.W. Pacific Highway
Tigard, Oregon 97223

Streamside Anglers
P.O. Box 2158
Missoula, Montana 59801

Dick Surette Fly Fishing Shop
P.O. Box 686
North Conway, New Hampshire
  03860

Tackle-Craft
P.O. Box 280
Chippewa Falls, Wisconsin 54729

Sources of Tools and Materials / 140

Tack-L-Tyers
939 Chicago Avenue
Evanston, Illinois 60202

Thomas & Thomas Company
4 Fiske Avenue
Greenfield, Massachusetts 01301

D. H. Thompson
335 Walnut Avenue
Elgin, Illinois 60120

Universal Imports
P.O. Box 1581
Ann Arbor, Michigan 48106

Yellow Breeches Fly Shoppe
Box 205, Route 174
Boiling   Springs,   Pennsylvania
    17007